ALLOW ME
New and Selected Poems
1975–2021

IRENE WILLIS

ALLOW ME:

NEW AND SELECTED POEMS
1975-2021

IRENE WILLIS

International Psychoanalytic Books (IPBooks)
New York • www.IPBooks.net

ISBN: 978-1-956864-17-5

for Olivia

ALLOW ME

Sudden and quiet, surrounded by friends
—John Milton's way—
But who gets to choose this ordered end
Trim and untattered, loved ones at hand?
    Allow me that day.

                —Maxine Kumin

CONTENTS

NEW POEMS   1

Maxine: Our Last Exchange	3
Interrupted	4
Time Rushes On	5
The Perfection of the Dead	6
Mirror	7
Emergency	8
We	9
She	10
Downsized	11
True Believer	12
Dame School	14
What They Taught	15
Language Deficit	16
To Dig the Sandy Shore	18
Whistling Girl	19
Rejection	20
Longhand	21
Last Book	22
Canine Love	23

Happy Dog 24

Tending 25

Victims 26

Abu Ghraib 27

Teenage Girls 28

Childhood Re-Imagined 29

Answer 30

Deceased 31

Almost There 32

We're All Winners Now 33

Donations 35

Hurrying 36

When You Live in a Place Like This 37

Hope 38

Afraid in the Age of Covid 39

Lost Poem 40

Cockles 41

SELECTED POEMS   43

THEY TELL ME YOU DANCED (1995)   45

Her Cane   47
They Tell Me You Danced   48
Becoming Hard of Hearing   50
Tenement Year   52
Dancing Feet   55
Aubade   57
On Dingle, County Kerry   58
Closing the Rented Cottage   59
Mornings   60

AT THE FORTUNE CAFÉ (2005)   61

Dereliction   63
Gender   64
At the Fortune Café   65
Lives of the Famous   66
If   68
Ashes   69
A Ghazal Afterword   71

THOSE FLAMES (2009)   73

Bitter   75

You Want It?   76

The First Time I Saw Death, I Laughed   77

Those Flames   78

Middle Distance   79

We Were Laughing Then   80

The Wilders   82

Ocean Grove, NJ 1944–1985   83

REMINDER (2014)   85

Good Book   87

Song   88

Relief (NYC, 1938)   89

Reminder   90

El Mundo   91

Now   93

Resurgent   94

Rehearsal (2018)   95

Her Self   97

Rehearsal   98

A New Book   99

Following   100

Taking Care   101

Josh   102

Hers   103

Climate of Opinion:
Sigmund Freud in Poetry (2019)   105

Always the Man Somewhere   107

What They Bring: The Poetry of
Migration and Immigration (2020)   109

What Are You?   111

Border   112

GREEN DIALOGUE (2020)   113

Maxine Gone   115
I Was the Girl Who Always Spoke   117
Depression Baby   118
The Letters in My Dream   119
The Slowest Step   120
House   122

FROM *NEW YORK QUARTERLY MAGAZINE*   125

Delilah   127

UNCOLLECTED POEMS   129

Paris, 1971   131
Obsession   134
Book Lust   135
Boola-Boola   136
Campus   137
Visit to a Colonial Museum   138
Hanging On   139
Lost Poem   140
How It Happened   141

FROM *COSMOPOLITAN* 145

I Know You, Cat 147

Letter to Heloise 148

About Time 149

TRANSLATIONS 151

FROM *PAROLE* BY JACQUES PRÉVERT 153

A Page of Writing 155

The Horse's Story 157

Family Life 159

The Message 160

ACKNOWLEDGMENTS 161

NOTES 163

ABOUT THE AUTHOR 165

NEW POEMS

MAXINE: OUR LAST EXCHANGE

In memoriam, Maxine Kumin (1925–2013)

My pipes froze, I said in an e-mail.
I left a window open by mistake.

Of course, she said. *Everyone knows when it's below twenty you
drain the pipes.*

I thought below zero, but no matter.
Did your Suzy get the revised poem I sent?

I gave it to her, she said, *but right now she's dealing with frozen
pipes herself.*

How did we sign off? I'll look it up. Luckily, I don't delete
too much

and anyway, I wouldn't delete Maxine.
I couldn't delete Maxine.

INTERRUPTED

This is the second
time in a decade
someone has said
*That was a long
time ago*, when I
called to say hello
after what seemed
like a brief
interruption.

She should be dead
by now, they must
abe thinking—or
at least, long gone.

Instead, here I am—
cell against my ear,
trying to finish
a sentence
on a moving sidewalk.

TIME RUSHES ON

Time, it is said, *marches* on
but why, when it's no parade?

Shakespeare said it *creeps.*
Yes, but *petty pace* is when we're young.

Now I find it *hastens, rushes*—
At least for me, Time, O Time

rushes on, *rushes* on.
rushes, rushes, rushes.

THE PERFECTION OF THE DEAD

Is there a way
to tolerate absence
except by perfecting
the dead?

Must the smart one
now be brilliant
the pretty one
beautiful
the talented gifted
because dead?

They haven't achieved
more anything
because of it.

What they have done
is die
which we
perhaps less bravely
(I'll give them that)

have not.

MIRROR

Is this what age does?
I don't look old, I think—
just worried and tired,
like the old actors on TV
who look as if they're
about to cry.

EMERGENCY

I gave them a green wool hat
to go with his green bathrobe

when they bumped him down
on the stretcher, dickory-dock.

As I jumped into the car to
follow, I thought of how

I had to keep him going—
tall grandfather clock

Husband—keep that
pendulum swing and heart

(good heart, strong, brave heart)
running, with its old *tick-tock.*

WE

Standing quite near
or even right here

is someone who's lost
a belov-ed.

This he or this she
can no longer say *we*

condemned to the realm of
I/me.

SHE

"Your deepest self
is always beside you,"
I read, turning to *her*
to whom I've been
talking all this time.

"As if I didn't know,"
I say sarcastically
knowing that She
unlike others
won't mind.

DOWNSIZED

I used to want
To stand out
As well-dressed
To make heads turn

But now that I've moved
Up here
I've right-sized myself
After the big
Downsizing
All I want
Is to blend in.
Today I gave away
My fancy fur coat
And slipped into
A black puffer for the cold.
The uniform of everyone
Up here
Where I live now
And will probably be Forever.

TRUE BELIEVER

More a believer than I knew
I'm trying *Genesis* again

First time since childhood
when Bible Stories for Children

sat on my shelf beside
A Child's Garden of Verses

Mother Goose and the fairy books
with names like Crayolas.

So here I go, deciding
as I did when on a diet

that limits carbohydrates
and sugary treats

to forego the fat pile
of books on my nightstand

for this new (and costly)
large-print King James

noticing, ever self-observant,
how I'm slowing down

before I pick it up
even as I try to ask you

Dear Sympathetic
(I hope) Reader,
if you can know *about* a book
without having read it?

Silly question, just marking time
before opening the first silky,

slithery (did you get that?) brand-new
and too-expensive page.

DAME SCHOOL

Downstairs to the kitchen
late night for a snack
I stumble across a sight
that nobody should see:
our mother cat, Ophelia,
six kittens circling her,
is carefully teaching them
how to dismember a mouse.

Gently, she takes the head
in her forepaws, then jaws.
Hearing a crunch that I can't bear
I race upstairs, ashamed—
for both of us, but more for me,
since it was I who'd tasted—
no, *bitten*—that apple long ago.

WHAT THEY TAUGHT

A lot was about eating:
don't butter a whole slice
then fold it in half
and stick it in your mouth.

Some was about faces:
don't make them
keep yours straight
no staring
or grimacing.

Some about stance:
hands off your hips
don't swing your arms
head up
when you walk.

Bedtime was a mystery:
hands outside the covers
But *why?*
I didn't want cold shoulders
even then.

LANGUAGE DEFICIT

Waiting outside the hair salon,
having called on my cell to be let in

I remember when *beauty parlor*
was where my mother went

to get her rollers, permanent
and henna treatments to look like red

trotting in with a big *pocketbook* or,
as she said, *pock-a-book*

whereas I, Miss Sophisticate,
carry an even bigger *handbag*

and young girls now
wear (heaven forfend) *backpacks.*

Dads, brothers, boyfriends
went to striped-pole *barbershops*

and steered clear of *fairylike* stylists,
still *verboten;* no one wanted to be a sissy

nor did anyone, even then, wear *spectacles,*
except in jest, when *eyeglasses*

were *au courant.* Oh, what to say
when I'm so out of it

as language races on?
Out-distanced now entirely

I flip my large-key Jitterbug,
feeling savvy, but still

not knowing how to
text or photograph

and using it only for outgoing calls
in yet-to-come emergencies,

I hang up my handicap plaque
and grab my cane

before my hairdresser, *sans* coat
but masked for the pandemic

comes out to help me in.

To Dig the Sandy Shore

My holes were empty like a cup.
In every hole the sea came up
Till it could come no more.

—*Robert Louis Stevenson*

At my grandparents' shore house
I was the proper child
Who sat on a horsehair sofa
And talked to the parrot in her cage.

My corseted Nana took me to the beach.
We sat under a huge striped umbrella.
Around us, children built sandcastles,
Screamed as they ran into waves.

Once, when her eyes were closed,
I ran after the others, voice rising
In a solo scream no one could hear.
A breaker carried me off......

WHISTLING GIRL

"Whistling girls and crowing hens
always come to some bad end,"
my grandmother kept saying
and saying as I tried—
but still I tried and tried
and no sound would come out
of my pursed lips until
in one of my story books
a man said, "I have to wet
my whistle."

So I grabbed a water glass,
took a sip, then another,
tried again and heard
a sound
like a small whistle.
A *whistle!*
And Nana heard me
and kept saying it
and saying it
until she died
and still I tried.

Can you hear me, Nana?
I'm whistling!

REJECTION

I remember my
shock when I
overheard my beloved father
saying he'd
never read a book
written by a woman.

Aspiring writer that
I was at ten, I didn't
stop, couldn't stop
but that was my first
rejection slip.

LONGHAND

To write a book in longhand—
as John le Carré did his first
while working as a spy
and diplomat
or even a poem in longhand
as I just did
seems to tax my
diminishing
capabilities.
In fact, signing my name
in readable longhand
seems almost
insurmountable.
I think about the root
of that word
as I scratch my way
up the last
mountain
with my left (and still left)
hand.

LAST BOOK

"This isn't your last one, Mom,"
my daughter said in an e-mail,

"Poetry is as natural to you
as breathing."

If so, I just breathed a poem
onto a lined, yellow page.

Reader, tell me: *Is* it?
I depend on you to know.

CANINE LOVE

"Don't anthropomorphize,"
a vet once told me
but how can I write about dogs
and *not?*

All we have to do
is look at their faces
the smiles and laughs
and sadness echoing

our own—no, not
echoing so much as
mirroring—if
a mirror had feelings

and a beating
warm heart.

HAPPY DOG

I love to think about my Abigail—
beautiful Springer who pulled me off my feet
when those big Golden Retrievers moved next door.
Abbie nearly broke my nose, but I've long since
forgiven her, as how could I not, since she never stopped
loving—me and everyone, including that woman
who had just lost her own. A friend visited her with
Abigail, who went right over and started kissing
and soon progressed to cuddling, and now they two
are one, and the woman thinks she's always owned her.
Both happy, and I'm glad, because fifty-one pounds
are too much for me, where I live now and probably
will be forever, old as I am. But, leashed, she's been seen
by both my daughter and me, I'm sure,
so must have had someone else to take her out.
Take her out has a resonance I don't like, but I remember
when, back at our house she had her doggie door
and big beautiful back yard, where she explored
and pooped to her heart's content. Happy, happy dog!

Tending

One could do worse than
be
a woman who tends
a man who loves
as he does.

VICTIMS

The stupid: people who start fires
accidentally.

The wicked: people who start fires
intentionally.

We are all victims
of the stupid and wicked.

Often the stupid
are victims of the wicked

But sometimes the wicked
are victims of the stupid

Which is why we are all
victims and victimizers

still burning
from the fire's raging path.

ABU GHRAIB

It took Botero to bring it home—
not the gray printed pages
of the *New York Times*
but the Colombian painter,
Fernando Botero, with his
bulbous hyper-reality—
balloon-like legs and arms,
gigantic pecs and torsos.
Botero, whose paintings,
even of the innocuous, held
a recipe for horror.
2003, therefore within
our adult and all-too-recent
memory, knowing that it was
in our name, with our dollars,
leaving us, now that the enabler
who lit the match is venerable,
venerated, decently retired.
Still, trying to read more,
learn more, I find I can't
even look. How easily we
learn to dis-remember here
in America the beautiful,
our Pilgrims' pride.

TEENAGE GIRLS

One stands up for climate change
and still stands up to the world—

Another takes the video
that leads to the conviction

of the cop who murdered
while children watched.

God bless the grandchildren.
We're jubilant today!

CHILDHOOD RE-IMAGINED

What a child I was
when I was a child
but of course that was
because I *was*.

At twelve I was excited
that we were at war
and would have loved
to point a gun.

The German delicatessen
man was a threat
as was the housekeeper
my mother relied on.

But by myself, I knew for sure
I could have won that war.

ANSWER

to May Swenson's "Question"

What can I do but focus now,
my body, my hound?
So much to do before I turn down
the light on these now withered arms,
still-robust legs, and cream
whatever parts I still can reach,
I read the obits with a laser eye to see
who of my lot will be the next to go.
This will happen, that I know
because "the Bible tells me so"—
a song I sang when I was two
I can't forget. Can *you?*

DECEASED

I'm writing this
after names
in my address book.
It's better than
crossing them out.

Who knows
when I might need them?

Hey, everybody:
mortality, remember?

O, you
heedless young.

ALMOST THERE

Gifts in tow, they tumble from the van,
nieces and nephews, ready to take a look,
now that I'm ancestral and they're grown.

Slowly, I've turned into the matriarch.
I feel it creeping up my legs like stone,
my knees now angled to the floor

in case a little one
should toddle in with something like a book
that must be read aloud to be understood,

with pictures for the looking and the turning,
like those in the big album I've uncovered—
the one with pages black from the beginning

and blurry snapshots sliding from their slots.

WE'RE ALL WINNERS NOW

"I want to be a famous poet,"
a friend said
and then I realized
she wasn't joking.

"As for me," my student said,
"I just want to be famous."

And so she went on Facebook
and other sites—
a budding Pia Zadora,
famous for being famous.

She made it with her postings
about where she was
what she had for lunch
who with
and what, famously,
she was or was not
wearing.

One friend managed
to make her cleavage
famous
another her hair—

both busy

establishing their brands
deciding they would be writers
and writing it in their blogs.

Why bother with
licking envelopes
typing e-mails
and waiting
for acceptance
and awards?

What matters
is what we think of ourselves
and convincing you
to agree.

DONATIONS

So much to think about
before we accept a gift.

How did donors *make*
the money they're gifting?

Did they inherit it?
Pay taxes? Use campaign funds?

Does it matter
and why?

How does a non-profit
stay one?

And about all this:
have we become *more* honest

or *less?* Oh, stop worrying.
Open your hands.

Who was it said
greed is good?

HURRYING

Trying to force myself
to slow down, take it easy,
rest

I have such a sense
of imminence, urgency,
haste

to get wherever it is
I think I want—no, *need*
to be

But *why?*
Is it age alone—
long-standing habit, what?

And who is doing this
performance review?

WHEN YOU LIVE IN A PLACE LIKE THIS

You don't have to be close
to draw comfort from people nearby.

It's enough to know someone's there—
a neighbor who sees you daily—

but now a van's parked at the curb.
When you live in a place like this

you watch them come and go—
sometimes to a care facility

or to their daughters'.
Always it's the daughters at the end.

When you live in a place like this
often it's an ambulance.

A new friend goes out on a gurney
and you're glad it isn't you.

HOPE

"Hope is not a medicine,"
the wise man says.

"Yet without it," I reply,
"no medicine
can do its work
and neither can I."

AFRAID IN THE AGE OF COVID

Fear Trumps recognition

when a masked nod

or wave

brings no response.

LOST POEM

The poem is gone.
The magazine is gone.
All I can remember is
The last few lines:
"The audience, as they say,
sat on its hands."
I am still
sitting on my hands.

COCKLES

I got a little note
from someone today
that warmed the cockles of my heart.
Although I have no idea
what cockles are
I surely must have some
because here's
another note
and already I can feel
my cockles growing warm.

SELECTED POEMS

I

THEY TELL ME YOU DANCED

(University Press of Florida, 1995)

HER CANE

On the day my mother decided to be old
she picked up a cane at the drugstore on the corner,
a heavy one, its handle curved like a bumbershoot,
rubber-tipped like a crutch, of dark-stained oak.

From that day forth, whenever she ventured out,
whether to take a bag of garbage to the incinerator
or to take a meal in the coffee shop downstairs
or to wait at the door of her building for a ride,

she carried her cane or leaned on it like a scepter.
It gave her dignity, an air of privileged handicap—
both of which she wore with great aplomb—
and best of all, from her point of view, I think,

enabled her to look down all the time instead of up.
I know, because I never, from the first day she used it,
saw the old, head-up stance she had faced the world with,
except in her own apartment, where she danced

to the door when the bell rang—a toilet flushing
behind her, a drawer slammed shut, the "TV off,
in case someone should want her, just in case
the doorbell ringing meant that someone did.

THEY TELL ME YOU DANCED

Here we go, my mother,
here we go, down the long
corridor to the white room
with the green chair hard
by the bed, its arms narrow,
the metal stool under it
waiting for your two feet
in their brown, clumsy boxes.
An afghan is folded
across the white spread
its flags of color pointing
to you, your sparse, red-brown
"touched-up" hair. No gray.
They tell me you danced
last night, surprising them
all in the all-purpose room
after the Shabbat
after the mass and vespers
after supper with the "alerts,"
as they call those of you
who still have your wits.
"Most of our guests,"
the director says,
"are pleasantly confused."
She tells me again how
you danced, glancing at you
with twinkling complicity.

You smile, cheekbones rising,
eyes not meeting mine, and
something furtive enters.
What did you do? Hootchie-
Kootchie? Shimmy? Shake?
Boogie? Sixties twist?
"She does a mean Charleston,"
I say, feeling somehow betrayed,
as if a family secret held
for years had just come out.
"Try *Ja-Da* sometime
on that old piano
and watch her move."
You, Mother, sit smiling
in your narrow chair,
 crochet hook waving
as you strain to hear.

BECOMING HARD OF HEARING

It's not hard; it's soft.
What happens is, the words
soften and wilt,
dissolve at the edges
into wisps that tease the ears
with illusion of meaning.
While meaning drifts,
hiding in crevices of smiles, winks, grimaces,
I try to ingest what's left:
imbroglio, panache, macaroni.
Rotund with vowels, these
are my ears' feast,
fat berries in a forest
where little grows
to fill my basket.
How strange that the baroque
is my inheritance—
Anglo-Saxon sharpness
gone the way of most acuity,
edges dulled on knives
that make things happen:
cut, do, best.
What I have now

are rainbow scarves,
lacy arabesques:
aroma, mellow, purple,
Honolulu, cherish.
I am learning
my mother's language
at last.

TENEMENT YEAR

This is where I belong, she must have thought,
taking the little girl in her clothes from Best's
and her perfect haircut, ribbon, Mary Janes
to the tenement with the toilet in the hall
and bathtub under a lid in the kitchen.

*This is where I belong. My mother lived
in a place like this and brought me up like this
and it's time my daughter learned,* she must have
thought when I was eight and my brother four,
still wetting and throwing tantrums.

This is where I belong, she seemed to say
as she leaned from the ladder, hammering nails
for curtain rods to dress our airshaft windows
with starched Priscillas, then fastening
tiebacks with white thumbtacks.

This is where we live, I told myself, *where Daddy
can't find us, where no one, not even
Nana and Grandpa, not even Grandma, Uncle
Max or the friends from our old neighborhood
can find us, where we're safe.*

This is where we belong. You mustn't tell
even the teacher at school, she said as she handed
me lunch and money for milk and subway fare
and told me which train to take uptown
to where the old neighborhood began.

This is how we belong; we mustn't tell,
said the subway train as I rode uptown
to where the old streets and Daddy were
and walked to school with my books and secret,
my secret and books, and still got stars.

Gold stars on top of all my papers
and tried to smile and didn't tell
and wanted Daddy to find us again
there in our second-floor hiding place
in the building on West 100th Street.

But when Grandma in her Persian lamb
and Uncle Max with the big cigar
showed up one day on our front stoop
my mother came out in her flowered robe
and said, *I told you not to come here.*

She said that to her own mother and brother.
I didn't know why, but then she said
Mrs. Schultz, the neighbor who helped us most,
and some of the other neighbors too
had talked about how they hated Jews.

I didn't know what being Jewish meant
because I went to Presbyterian Sunday School.
But when that fat girl pushed me on the stairs
that led to the basement gym in our old school

and called me dirty Jew the day I got the most

stars ever,

I almost knew.

DANCING FEET

I want my dancing feet, my mother said,
surprised by tears on my living-room couch
as Fred and Ginger tangoed on the tube—
her own feet strangers on the ottoman,
strapped and buckled in fake leather
molded to fit bunions, hammertoes, corns,
This was the lady who used to do the shimmy
and the Charleston, who fox-trotted her way
into one marriage and out, then met another
husband at a dance and took the measure
of him by his two-step.
I stood up, moved to music for her,
swinging into an elegant solo dip
worthy of chiffon, rhinestones, marcel wave.
She bobbed and clapped. *You always were
a good dancer.* Unbidden as they were unworn,
the tap shoes surfaced in my mind again,
nested in tissue, patent leather shiny, dark,
ties of grosgrain ribbon, and on toes and heels
the marvelous metal that set them apart
from Sunday Mary Janes and schoolday Oxfords.
Every time I took them down those days
it was to admire, try on, admire, put back,
the lessons long since over.
Attrition or absence, it was all the same.
Where Olga Gazarian's School of the Dance
was, I wasn't. It was either shoes or lessons,

not both. What did I want—blood from a
turnip? Camp *and* uniforms?
So I grew up, as she must have every bit
intended me to. Got some sense in my head.

AUBADE

Taped chimes
from the church with the dummy steeple
down past the boutiques and shopping mall.
Daylight through orange curtains.
On the far wall, a picture:
together in a dinghy a grandfatherly sea captain
and a small girl.
He lets her hold an oar.
Proud of her power but fearful,
she stares from the frame for answers,
I have none.
The air conditioner throbs.
Beside me, you stir in your sleep and reach.
I turn, dreaming waves.

ON DINGLE, COUNTY KERRY

Walking away from the burden of who I am
down a dirt road on Dingle, I see myself.
I see us, you and me, from the back.

I see our packs, bulging with the oddments
of our profession of being who we are:
the ones who carry ourselves wherever we go.

Wild thyme scents the air, small black flies
circle our heads; the dirt underfoot is quiet,
Stealthily, we walk past a farmhouse, a fence.

A dog comes out, barking in Mother Goose,
The road is a lane, the gate a stile
and you, whose head is a foot above mine

in its separate packet of purple-scented air
are my fancy. I am your locket, your love,
your tuffet, your curds, your whey.

The Ireland of our fathers, yours and mine,
waits like a pocket, open to catch us,
plucked from the lane like two pennies.

CLOSING THE RENTED COTTAGE

We stack chairs on the deck, turn valves,
bag trash for the dump, up-end the outdoor table,
do one last load of wash, hang up the broom,

check to see there's nothing left that's ours
and leash the dogs for one last amble up
our borrowed hill. Later we'll fold blankets,

pile pillows on the naked bed and pack
a lunch for the road with what's left
in the fridge, Now we watch our own two dogs

sniff rented leaves, eat neighbors' grass,
deposit fat turds in the center of the road—
suburban decorum lost in this silence.

Not owning a blade of this grass, a stick of that house,
we taste the freedom of the dispossessed.
Closing so carefully, we can open.

MORNINGS

I wake and stretch.
Two dogs bloom at my sides.
I study the dogs now
as I once studied
my face in the mirror
and the child
bending to the flower.

II

At the Fortune Café

(Snake Nation Press, 2005)

DERELICTION

Remember the uncle who started things
but never finished them? Abandoned siding,
books with nothing on, no wall behind,
tiles without their mastic, moldering grout,
creeping mildew—a small spot first, like that
mole with uneven color and irregular edges
the articles are always warning us about?
When I went back to see the house
our tenants had so abruptly left, I found
shutters awry, as if they'd lost their minds,
a dead animal in the drive, its head and body
split so that I couldn't find its pride and
bearing and all my shining dulled. I felt,
instead of anger, shame—a strong, suffusing blush—
as if it had been I who did it all:
unhinged the shutters, let them fall,
let mail and papers pile up at the door,
beheaded that small corpse and left it there.
I felt the way that uncle should have felt
or must have felt, or didn't, he who couldn't
see what others saw, the dereliction
of neglect, of letting down, turning away.

GENDER

The old dog puzzles hers.
Locked by spaying at six months
into eternal childhood
a romping toddler still
despite her waddle and her breath,
the dance of her ears *memento mori*.
We take the parenthood from our pets
the way they bound my breasts
when he was born
the way they bind the feet
to make of femininity
a mincing masquerade
the way the clitoris is excised still
to punish joy
hands placed outside covers
tied at the sides
hacked off at the wrists,
The way the child is silenced
with words that box the ears,
the bark is muted
and the yelp of pleasure dulled.

AT THE FORTUNE CAFÉ

The woman with red hair in a topknot,
white face, black necktie
places our check on the table
beside my coffee cup
and I see that her hand
is tipped with playing cards,
Queen of Diamonds on her thumb
Jack of Hearts on her ring finger
Ten of Spades across the nail
that tips the pinkie
on the hand she uses now
to pour out refills.
I ask her and she tells us how
she sat last night in the nail salon
where the Queen of Hearts
plied her meticulous trade—
ran a tiny brush around each cuticle
dipped a tiny brush and dipped again
till Fortune smiled from ten perfect moons.

LIVES OF THE FAMOUS

I leave the store
and a voice calls out behind me
from a book.
It's Auden, still talking after all these years.
Now it's something about
accessible, democratic,
the language of everyday.
Well, well, I think,
remembering his face
across the table
at the White Inn,
Fredonia, New York,
a dried plum, too long in the sun.
An undergraduate asked
to chair the lecture series,
I had begun to fulfill my destiny
as a footnote in the lives
of the famous, a dot
at the bottom
of an exclamation point
punctuating
a minor anecdote:
Whittaker Chambers
hunched over his desk at *Time,*
his wire IN basket
where his OUT should be,

left side switched to right
before I, bold copygirl, pointed it out.
Grunting, he let me move them,
but that night switched them back!

IF

If we get old
I say to my husband
as we drive up the hill,
where will we go,
what do?

If, we say, *if,*
afraid to admit
what we know full well
is true.

We shift gears and down
the pine trees whistle,
the grasses blow.
We go. We go.

ASHES

I can remember when I didn't know
what death was.
Here in New England
I pass it every day.
A cemetery beside the supermarket,
another on the way to the beauty shop,
and on the road to the doctor's office
three more.
One in front of a farmhouse:
three white markers in the yard
where the other afternoon
a man and two young boys
were digging.
Last night I stood in my own yard
and saw the Dipper clearly overhead.
This morning where I walked
the sky was an upturned blue bowl
and I was inside it
as the earth moved slowly
with me on it, walking.
I remember reading of a tree
whose apples grew fat and ripe
as its roots followed the line
of a body buried beneath it
and of a poet who paid homage to her dog
by tasting its ashes.

I remember a friend
who kept his lover's ashes
in a teapot
and another who spoke of her husband's
with erotic intensity,
And then there was me,
who didn't want my brother's
scattered from a mountain in Montana
or buried beside a highway in Vermont
and who now begins to remember
how we all held hands and sang
and how, laughing, we all fell down.

A GHAZAL AFTERWORD

When my grandmother died, she thought I had turned my
 back.
What I said might have helped her go; what I say can't bring
 her back.

When my father's heart broke, I thought, *Why didn't he call me?*
surely I, of all others, could have held him back.

When my brother left his life, I saw him out the door
like someone who was sure he would be back.

When my mother gripped my hand, we crossed the busy street
to buy me shoes again; sidewalk mica shone on our way back.

My name is Peace; sun drowned my eyes. I wore
a cardboard crown with feathers when I came back.

III

THOSE FLAMES

(Bay Oak Publishers, Ltd., 2009)

BITTER

Aloes for my brother's thumb,
Antabuse for my father
Argyrol for my colds and her quinsies.

Here comes my mother with the bitter brush.
My mother, the bitter lady,

giving us all our medicine.

YOU WANT IT?

Here, take it,
my mother would say,
unwinding a scarf
from her neck,
slipping off a bracelet,
the ring too small for my finger
she tried to force anyway.
A giver, a couldn't-hold-
on-to-it, my mother was.
She would give you,
as they say,
the shirt off her back—and ours.
My father's three-piece
suit and gray fedora, my
white embroidered sweater,
last year's coat, and once,
three jackets, lowered
on the dumbwaiter
when the super needed clothes,
A fiver for the insurance man,
out of cigars. Hazel,
my mother's friend, got *me,*
for lessons on an out-of-tune
piano while her out-of-work
husband sat in my father's
pants and watched.

The First Time I Saw Death, I Laughed

My friend's Aunt Edna lay against
a mound of pillows on a bed
in their front room, where she had lain
as long as I had known that house.
There to play, we always saw her first.
Sometimes the covers moved; now they didn't.
Aunt Edna's face was powdered white:
her lips were pink; so were the nails
on her thin fingers folded on the quilt.
My best friend knelt to pray; I knelt
to hide my face inside my handkerchief.
I gave them all I had at ten to offer:
fear and laughter, Later, I was praised.
My shaking shoulders, hidden face
—had passed for grace.

THOSE FLAMES

Attuned to the change,
I'd watch my father's face
for the slurring, subtle shift,
the languid tongue
that signaled the unraveling
I'd come to know, at six,
as *drunk* from the "cup of tea"
he'd wink at a waiter for
or the tall bottle of ale
he'd down as cigarettes
lingered in the ashtray
on our kitchen table.
Drunk would drive my mother
out to a neighbor's or
into the street, leaving me
to listen to the rant.
My job. She gave it to me.
Unwatched, he'd "burn
the house down," just as
she feared I would
if I plugged in the iron,
turned on the stove.
Together, my father and I
would bring on that
incendiary, those flames.

MIDDLE DISTANCE

Open-handed, glad to be here
buying a paper
with the change from his breakfast,
he wants to linger, chat her up a bit
before pushing out the door
near the register and cigarette machine,
but the cashier's mastered the stare
of the middle distance
three feet from where his face is—
over where the Pennysavers
and the real estate giveaways
are more interesting
than this old guy
who's got Florida written all over
his golfing face and tee-shirt.
Even his visor is more of a draw,
the flick of her wrist says
as she counts out four ones, two quarters.

WE WERE LAUGHING THEN

...to write poetry after Auschwitz
is barbaric

    —Theodor Adorno

But we were laughing then.

In World War II my father was overseas,
writing me a V-mail letter every day
with words blacked out—and places—
but with funny pictures in the margins.
That was all I knew.
In Junior High School 52
we were reading *Ivanhoe*
and taking parts to read aloud.
My blonde friend Ellen
was Rowena.
Rose Red, and Snow White.
When we went up front to read
the biggest boys in class
who always sat in back
made faces at us, and we laughed.
I was sent out of the room
for "inappropriate laughter"
and got demerits and a D in conduct
while my father was earning
a Good Conduct medal
and a Purple Heart.

What did we know of Auschwitz?
What did anyone know? Did Vannie,
our German housekeeper, know—
or her husband, the butcher?
Did my teachers, Miss Bernstein
or Mr. Gold? What about M. Clement,
who sent me out of the room
for wearing lipstick in that terrible school
where the only good thing was our laughter?

Did my Jewish mother know,
who paid Vannie every month
from my father's hundred-dollar
allotment check?

But we were laughing then.
if there were tremors, like before a quake,
we didn't know or couldn't have known
or might have heard or should have heard
goose-steps under the earth,
rising to our ears and filling them with blood.

THE WILDERS

They got their rocks off first at Highbridge Pool,
circling girls like sharks and ripping tops off.
Later came the bottoms, while the lifeguards

looked the other way and trained binoculars
on the highest dive, in case somebody
in trouble needed saving right away.

In Central Park they stripped a young woman bare
who had come to New York City to see the sights.
Her honeymoon. She hid behind her husband,

who cowered. They had knives, and teeth they showed
in grins that foretold mayhem, unrestrained
down paths designed by Olmsted for their grace.

Soon their lives would change;
they'd be recruited
like kids who came from shanties in the woods
or off the farms where they were slopping pigs.

They'd learn *salute* and *Sir* and breaking in
with sticks and guns to homes where
grown men huddled
and women clutched books to hidden hearts
books they said were holy, like the prayer books
these books carried to their First Communions.
One crossed himself before he opened fire.

OCEAN GROVE, NEW JERSEY: 1944–985

All stories, if you carry them
far enough, end in death.

  —Ernest Hemingway

Polly died, choked on a bit of soapstone
from her new feeding dish
with Grandpa's song, my laugh and hello
and Nana's shrill demands
trapped in her voicebox.

Grandpa died, a heart attack on his
way back from the Victory Garden,
where he dug and hoed
and brought back vegetables
for her to put up, wet pack,
in the steaming kitchen.

He cursed her on his deathbed,
Aunt Flo said, lying in what
became hers after Nana died,
cursing him, my father, all of us,
Flo holding back what she knew for
fear Nana would reach
from the grave to find her.

And finally the dogs, "Put to sleep"
by the estate lady whose job it was
to auction off the furniture for

the doctor who was willed the house
when Nana disinherited us.

So be it. Years later, the house
was bought by a builder, who
gutted it, tricked up the outside,
razed the blue hydrangeas, put in
a microwave and a trash compactor
and called up the adperson whose
notice I read in the *New York Times*.
Drawn in, we went, my new husband
and I, with ready cash. An hour later
I stood in the room I'd slept in last
when I was ten, after walking from
the station holding Grandpa's hand.
Now, through the open window,
I could almost smell the taffy, hear
waves crashing down on the boardwalk.

But it didn't work. I wanted Polly,
screaming for her morning coffee.
I wanted the whatnot in Grandpa's room,
with the arrowheads and seashells.
I wanted the horsehair sofa in the parlor
and Nana saying, "Do you want scallops?
I have some fresh," and showing me
where my towels were.

IV

Reminder

(Word Poetry, 2014)

GOOD BOOK

for Alicia Ostriker

Begat/begat/begat
Smote/smote/smote

Strife/slaughter
Slaughter/strife

Begat.
Blessed/blessed.

Smite. Beget.

SONG

We love who gives us song...
a line from one of my own old poems
remembers how they sang around the flat—
even my brother, on bended knee,
doing his Jolson *Mammy* at thirteen.
My father, when he was sober, sang
Little Brown Jug, with its laughing refrain—
a *ha* that sounded real, that sounded home.
The *you* was me, I knew, in *you and me.*
How I love thee was the part I waited for
and made me beg to have it sung again.
I was *thee* then still, the way I was
under the quilt with bears when I was small
and my mother sang in her high, soft voice,
Sleep, my little one, and I couldn't close my eyes
until I heard the words. I was her *pretty one,*
she sang, as I was his *thee,* and they were love.

RELIEF (NYC, 1938)

We used to know
Which kids were "on relief"
because they all wore
the same coats:
one year, spotted black and white
like Dalmatians,
another, electric blue.

But it was the furniture
that shocked—on the sidewalk
when a family was "evicted":
armchairs waiting
for somebody to sit down,
beds and couches piled
like all the boxes,
here and there a photograph,
framed and smiling

or serious as the girl
in my old white sweater
at the fourth-grade bake sale,
walking slowly, with one
small cookie.

REMINDER

When I say guess what happened—
my usual way of starting a story—
I see a look of alarm in his eyes,
replacing the sweet smile with which
he starts the iambic of our days—
our remaining days, which of course
everyone has—all that remains
is all we have—but when I say this
and know he still loves, it's as good
as the afternoon I came home earlier
than expected and said to this man
who can no longer walk with ease
and who spends his days in a chair
with his feet uplifted, when I said
as a joke, I half-expected to find you
jumping and dancing, he said,
not smiling, that's exactly how
I see myself in dreams.

EL MUNDO

My daughter and I found it—
the exact spot.
She knew it from the stonework overhead.
The theater marquee was gone
and the sign across the street that once said
DANCING now said EL MUNDO.
I stood under it, at my new age,
having lived a world of time since my fifth year,
having been and done whatever there was
since the day I held that small snow shovel
in the Broadway slip of park around the corner from my
grandparents' house of West 147th.

I never studied Spanish, but I know
That *world* is softened, easier in Romance:
le monde, le mondo, el mundo open
out in ways that *welt, varld, velt* do not.
Vowels go down easily, like Jell-O, Junket,
soft-boiled egg and milk—nursery foods
when my whole world was *dulzura, dolcezza*
and my mother thought I was adorable.

I stand here again in the January sun
as I did that winter afternoon
when Grandpop snapped the photo I still have.
And now my grown child kneels to get a shot
while the taxi driver waits at his yellow door.

When did I stop being *adorable?*
Was it when my mother saw me on the street
holding hands with that boy—what was his name?
Angie, I think, short for *Angelo.* Thirteen to my twelve.
She took one look at him and said to me, "Get upstairs,'
and to him, "Go home," as if to a dog. Was it because
she knew he wouldn't grow up to be like Dr, Bostwick,
who rented my grandparents' third-floor room—or any
doctor at all. Was it because he wrote me a letter
that she opened?

What is the look I have today in the camera's eye,
wrapped in my long black coat and red scarf?
Bewildered? Triumphant? Amazed?
To find myself here, after all these years,
in the modest company of my one child,
EL MUNDO behind me like a shade.

NOW

I still send Christmas cards with little notes
to those I hear from once a year, but now
hedge all my bets by saying, "Hope
this finds you well and happy," just in case
they're dead already when my envelope
arrives to tell them I'm still not.

Some women, now no longer slim or hot,
wear scarves to hide bald heads; their men
no longer hear at all from underground
or in the river where their ashes cry
for those of us who manage to hold on,
hoping next year's card won't find us gone.

RESURGENT

Now when I rise to greet each day
as if it were the same

of course it isn't
and yet it is—

every day so much like
another

I hardly know
which one it is—

or month—

but the year,
of course—

2020!

V

REHEARSAL

(IPBooks, 2018)

HER SELF

The self exists within the objects it has cherished,
to be resurrected there'

    –*Christopher Bollas*

And so, *her* mother's egg cup of plain white
china on a kitchen shelf beside my mother's
cream pitcher with hand-painted ivy and the
hidden crack that always spilled its contents
as she did secrets. In my dresser drawer
the tiny knitted booties with stitched-on pearls
that her best friend Nellie made for her when
she was old, and at my back door now, her cane.
Warming my knees, the jewel-toned afghan
she herself crocheted with skill she didn't
seem to have when I was growing up.
Can it be that she is here, hidden within egg cup,
pitcher, booties, afghan? Mother—*here?*
I think I've always known. Lately, I see her
everywhere. Driving by, hair the same permed
reddish-brown. Walking with the cane, holding
onto a daughter's arm. Seated in a restaurant,
(cheekbones, nose, the angle of her chin).
Why now, when she's been gone so long?
What objects will hold *me,* my own end near?

Rehearsal

My husband is reading
How We Die (Nuland)
Nothing to Be Frightened of (Barnes)
and *Mortality* (Hitchens)
and the dog is watching him
the dog with gray muzzle and eyebrows
is watching him.
My husband reads cheerfully
and I, who bought the books
he chose from my shelf,
am watching him and the dog.

A NEW BOOK

When he finishes
the books on death,
I give my husband
a book about life:
Travels with Epicurus
by Daniel Klein,
who traveled
to a Greek island
where very old men
sit in the sun, play cards
and tell each other
stories—which,
as Muriel Rukeyser said
(and now some scientists
agree) are what the universe
is really made of.
The listeners
already know the stories
but it doesn't matter
or perhaps it matters
because they do.
They talk and listen,
face to face,
drink glass after glass
of ouzo and sun.

FOLLOWING

I think I'm following you
I said to my beloved
into old age.

I've been waiting for you,
he said, holding out
his hand.

TAKING CARE

I didn't know it would be like this
but what I know now is

every day he comes downstairs
alive, I count myself lucky.

Is this what "taking care of" means?
If so, it's okay.

I take care.
He lets me.

JOSH

Old, we rely on people
to "help us out," as they say—
but really to do *whatever*,
which is most, that we can't
do ourselves. I get up early
to let in the furnace man
and, to my surprise, it's Josh,
the one who cuts our grass
and blows our leaves away.
Winters, he's our shoveler
now that Harry's gone.
And when we push the button
on our "Link to Life,"
I daresay the one who
shows up at the door
won't be a stranger, either—
might be Josh.

HERS

At some point after he died
she started to own her own life.

What did it mean, to own a life?
She couldn't explain it, but she knew

who she was, was not who she had been;
where she was, was not the same.

If she woke in that house, the house was hers;
if she slept there now, it was where she was.

If the bed was hard, she could up and leave.
If the bed was soft, it was hers to change.

If she saw him now, her mind was still.
But her mind was hers, and hers alone.

VI

CLIMATE OF OPINION: SIGMUND FREUD IN POETRY

(IPBooks, 2019)

ALWAYS THE MAN SOMEWHERE

1

Always the man is somewhere
other than where
I am.
When I am in Paris he is in London.
When I am in London
    he is in New York.
      When I am on the East Coast
      he is on the West.
Always
somewhere
delivering non-messages
keeping mailboxes empty
snowing the channel
making static on the line.

2

That he is somewhere
that his voice plays its tape in my head
keeps me from seeing
the man beside me at the counter
    or the next table
    on the plane seat
    or the bed.

3

Always the man somewhere
the man I cannot say good-by to
the man I am always saying
      good-by to.

4

Carefully he looks at me.
From the side of his eye
he looks at me
weighing the possibilities.
I sense him there
and weigh the possibilities
after he leaves.
When it is too late
I try to call him back
but he has been temporarily
disconnected.

VII

WHAT THEY BRING:
THE POETRY OF
MIGRATION AND IMMIGRATION
CO-EDITED WITH JIM HABA

(IPBooks, 2020)

WHAT ARE YOU?

What *are* you?
Was the first question
the kids in my new neighborhood—
in every one of my new neighborhoods—
would ask, right after, What's your name?

The first time, I didn't know
what they meant. I was eight
and new at this.

A person, I'd say. A human being.
A girl. What do you *think* I am?
You know what we mean, they'd say.
What nationality?

American, I'd say. I'm American.

They'd laugh. You can't be.
Nobody is. You have to be
something.

BORDER

"A 'Heartbreaking' Scene at the Border:
A Toddler Found Wandering Alone"
–*NY Times*, April 25, 2019

If reporters have their
hearts broken
can yours be broken too,

poor reader, trying to eat your
breakfast while that 3-year-old
has none—

your fingers smudged from
newsprint when the toddler's
are filled with grit?

Questions for the soul or intellect—
where to begin as we gulp our coffee
scarf down toast

carefully reach for vitamins to swallow
with water fresh from the tap
supplements for God-given nutrients

sustenance, abundance, wealth.

VIII

GREEN DIALOGUE

(IPBooks, 2020)

Maxine Gone

In memoriam, Maxine Kumin

1925–2014

How did we end it? Was I just a fan—
or truly a friend? I thought the latter

but did it matter if the tone was right:
not lofty, hierarchical, no slight ever

only gracious, warm response
to my gentle inquiries as to health,

animals, families, mutual friends,
and always immediate? She said once

that she saved all her e-mails
in a long cardboard box just like

the ones my father's shirts came in—
perhaps her father's too, or husband's

and it felt so familiar, even cozy,
I decided *friendship* was the word

whether she would acknowledge it or not.
Did any of our exchange, I wonder,
go to Bienecke's archive with the rest
or did they stay in that long shirt box

above her desktop computer
like the basket where I store mine?

Which would be better?
I hope, somehow, the latter.

I Was the Girl Who Always Spoke

–for Maria Mazziotti Gillan

Jolley was my name
till marriage pushed me
to the end of the alphabet.
But in second grade
a teacher told me it *wasn't*.
When she first called our names
she read mine as Joly (long o),
so I raised my hand
as I had been taught to do
and—taking a breath—
corrected her—*corrected
a teacher.*
"It's Jolley," I said.
"No, it's NOT!" she shouted.
"Jolly means to be happy.
Your name is Joly! (again with the long o).
I gasped, face hot. Kids who knew me gaped.
Lunchtime, I ran home crying.
I knew my name. I know I knew my name.
And to the end of my days
I will not forget yours, Miss Holweg.

Depression Baby

To open a new tube of toothpaste
after squeezing the old one
and rolling it tight.
To re-use a paper bag—long before
plastic started choking whales
and turtles.
To never spay our dogs and cats
because we didn't know about that
or even ticks.
We knew about mosquitoes, though,
and kept picking at the scabs.
Did we know about contagion at all?
Maybe not, because we got
every childhood disease
and (some of us) adult ones
we were too young to understand.
So the world was a mystery
but we celebrated
small triumphs
I remember as I throw away
another rolled-up, squeezed out
toothpaste tube.

THE LETTERS IN MY DREAM

Waking, I realized
I had been writing to my father,
telling him all that had happened
in the forty years since he died—
all in *my* life, that is, not the world's
because I figured he already knew
about that. Smart man, he'd be
120 now—so he must be really dead
despite my misgivings at the morgue
that I'd buried a stranger—one without
the scar on his chin I wouldn't let them
shave his beard to find.
If he were still alive
I would have heard from him, I know.
His last words, that landlady wrote,
were, *I have a daughter.*

THE SLOWEST STEP

I dreamt I saw my mother in the room
but first the slowest step I ever heard—

tap, tap, tap—until

the door creaked open; there she stood,
a dachshund running fast to greet

as if he knew her. "Is that your dog?"
I asked.

"No, *mine*," a voice behind me said,
(the relative I was visiting that day)

and now it was beginning to get dark,
yet here she was, first time since '93

One hundred thirteen years and there she stood,
out of breath but whole—somehow alive

while we were drinking tea and waiting
for my grandfather, due to arrive soon, too.

The slowest step had brought her here to us.

"I couldn't understand the conductor," she said,
"When he was telling me about the field."

Apparently, she'd crossed a field to get here.

"Mommy!" I cried. "Would you like a cup of tea?"

Still slow of step, she hobbled to the couch,
sat down beside us. I got up; she stayed.

If Grandpa came at last, I never knew.

HOUSE

Back at the house that used to be
my house

there will be a closed dog door
Invisible Fence still in the ground

fighting the grass once more
for status

my flowers—rhododendrons
already in bloom

soon upright lilacs, big-headed dahlias
drooping over the fence

and neighbors calling the man
to open the pool.

I would be saying hello to all
on my walk

The postman would be at our box
with lots of mail

and my husband, still in his chair,
phone at his side

so he could lead me home
from where I am now

in the middle of nowhere
everywhere.

From *New York Quarterly* Magazine: (1989)

DELILAH

Most women would rather have someone
whisper their name at the optimum moment than rocket with contractions
to the moon.

   —Merle Shain

The fat ones say my name
the thin ones don't and I
wonder what in their fatness
makes them linger over the I's
in my sound fill their mouths
with this sound of me till
my name coming out is a vial
of oil poured till I am swimming
in the slippery sea of my own
name and what
in the leanness of
the leanest ones
makes them parsimonious
even with this—swallowing
rather than say it filling
their mouths with air when I
am there beside them—there needing the sound of my name
in my air in my ear
to affirm.

IX

Uncollected Poems and Translations

PARIS, 1971

What am I afraid of
here in this strange city
where my child has gone
to meet the day alone?

Do rooftops threaten?
Will chimney pots
eat his fourteen years
iron balconies rub
the bloom from his cheeks
doorways unsettle
windows beckon
checked tablecloths
smother his verity
his charm?

Will he come to harm?
Drown in a puddle, perhaps—
felled by an elbow
a stranger's jostle, tickle,
who knows what?

Will he, having walked
his mile, still come home?

2

Near my bench in the garden
a Black American talks
with eloquence and dignity
to a woman with a brown sweater
and auburn hair.
His pipe is white
with a yellow stem,
his socks dark blue.
Her nose is acquiline.
Her hair has shine and grace.
Upstairs in the white space
of a white room
Van Gogh's sunflowers bloom
a darker gold than I expected.
The gold, the black, the man
from my home country
are a treat my eyes give me.
Eroticism seeds here
under the trees.
I want to sit like
a plant with consciousness.

3

The gentle rain that fell all day
washed the sky and hung
it outside our window
beside the flower-pot chimneys
the blue smock
and the *glissade* from
someone's piano.

OBSESSION

The man who comes to stanch my basement flood,
unclog the sump pump, clear the sodden mess
thinks I have a fetish, so he says,
for books that should be Kindled. "Save the space
for something else, like playspace for the kids."

What now? What this, when text is noun and verb
and Kindle brings no memory of sparks
or smoky ruins, only something good,
high-tech, bold, modern, up-to-date—
more so than I, clinging to copyright?

The books, thank God, are safe; I say a prayer
to whom or what protects the likes
of me, my submerged self recalled
in drowning hunks of paper on the floor.
O merciful, O muse, bereft and waiting

for drying out and blessed sublimating.
"A *fetish,*" he says, suggesting the erotic.
Did he see my burning Sappho on the shelf,
Catullus lingering behind
my lusty Shakespeare, prim Eliza. Barrett
nuzzling Sylvia, Robert, Anne—
confessionals lined up like penitents—
my shame, my bliss, my not-so-hidden sins?

"No," I say, "Your Honor, hip-booted savior.
"Obsessive is more accurate, I think."

BOOK LUST

I'm grabbing, gobbling books—
so many that want to be read,
that I want to read, lust for

so much I rape their shelves.
Where I've been is a locust trace
naked of jackets or bindings.

Pages and pages of print,
toothsome, delicious. Dusty
fingers scurry and smudge

like book mice, scavengers
savaging my hasty life.

BOOLA-BOOLA

My mother put on lipstick with her pinky,
dipped from a tiny pot beside the sink.

Eyes narrowed, she would smile to raise
her cheekbones, dip two fingers more for rouge.

She dusted powder with a feathery puff
that left her scent behind in the bathroom,

the place a lady went to "powder her nose"
or straighten seams on wrinkled rayon stockings

held up by garters dangling from a girdle or daringly from a
belt that showed her "private"

unless she pulled on what were then called "panties," the sub-
ject of much locker-room discussion

and object too of raids on dormitories—
headlined like the tales of swallowed goldfish.

CAMPUS

On the first day of the last term
a young man rushed into my room
and said "I can't stay here."

My innocent question brought it out:
"I just stopped a rape!" he said,
"and now I can't stay here."

On the next day of the last term
I checked my class list one more time
and waited for him to re-appear

and waited for him to re-appear.

VISIT TO A COLONIAL MUSEUM

I could have worn a dress like this, she thought;
this linsey-woolsey has a country feel,

a touch to savor, butter-churned, not woven—
maleness in its nub, and turkey-red

to warm the body on a winter morning.
This reel of history, summer-segment, mended

out of passed and re-passed other times,
gives all the lie to books. Who was it said

the Colonists were sober? I know better.

HANGING ON

Now that my New York friends
are down to size two
or vanished into zero

and talk about having had
"a little work done" I
wonder what I can do

as the leaf blower
whines outside my window.

LOST POEM

The poem is gone.
The magazine is gone.
All I can remember is
the last few lines:
"The audience, as they say,
sat on its hands."
I am still
sitting on my hands.

How It Happened

The villagers
torched the building,
They cleared the space
and made a park
and the body
of the murder victim
went into a casket
fit for a child.
The neighbors
brought flowers:
white for her purity,
pink for her girlhood
and what made her
want to hold a puppy
cradled against the buds
on her chest.
When the bad thing happened
and there was nothing t
hey could do to bring her back
they performed the ritual.
They exorcised
and sanctified
and then went home.
But they couldn't sleep
and neither could
what they had driven out.

It found a home
in someone by the river
who burned the body
of a man asleep on a bench
and when they caught
the one who did it
and stamped him out like a bug
what they had tried to kill
flew out in a million pieces.
Some became ants
That swarmed over another man
because he was black.
Some became bullets
that went into the chamber
of a homeowner's pistol.
Some became gunpowder
that teenagers fed to a pit bull
to make him mean.
Some turned into maggots
in the flesh of the dismembered.

Some went into statehouses
and flew in and out
of the mouths of orators
and the villagers
who had long since
burned out the flames
of their torches
and stamped out the embers
of what they had burned
took up their dead sticks
and used them as clubs.

FROM *COSMOPOLITAN:* (1975)

I Know You, Cat

Sit with pointed ears and watch me,
       Cat.
I'll show you that
I know your leanings.
Know curve of haunch
and sinewed tail.
Pink tongue licking fur,
fear of dogs' night barking,
sudden sounds, harsh movements.
Know hunger's stirring in the belly,
suckling young and nuzzling warmth,
rub against the ankle.
Know all the hiding places:
nests and boxes, cupboards,
chests of drawers,
hand stroking where it feels good
and cream.
Know liking to be alone sometimes
and definitely not alone other times
and always the readiness for pleasure,
erotic or otherwise.
I know you, Cat.

LETTER TO HELOISE

After the loving breaks,
when the body still fits in curve
of arm or thigh
but the loving is broken,
how do you
Elmer's Glue-it
Household Mend-it
Band-aid
Clorox
White-all Tide?
Dear Heloise,
who can answer all
household questions,
tell me please,
when the loving breaks
after All,
what do you do?

About Time

You with your yesterdays
and me with my tomorrows
make a good pair.
We lie here together,
you thinking: why couldn't it have been yesterday?
Me thinking:
why can't it be tomorrow as well
and the day after?
While today lies between us
like a neglected child.

TRANSLATIONS

FROM *PAROLE* BY JACQUES PRÉVERT

Page d' Écriture by Jacques Prévert

tr. Irene Willis

A PAGE OF WRITING

Two and two four
Four and four eight
Eight and eight sixteen ...
Repeat! says the teacher:
Two and two four
Four and four eight
Eight and eight sixteen.
But look! A lyrebird
is passing in the sky
the child sees it
the child hears it
the child calls out:
Save me
play with me
bird.
Then the bird comes down
Two and two four...
Repeat! says the teacher
and the child plays
and the bird plays with him...
Four and four eight
eight and eight sixteen
and sixteen and sixteen, what do they make?
They make nothing

and especially not thirty-two
in any way
and they go on.
The child has hidden the bird
in his desk
and all the children
hear its song
and all the children
hear its music
and eight and eight around they go
and four and four and two and two
around they go and out they go
and one and one are neither one nor two
one and one are equal
and the lyrebird plays
and the child sings
and the teacher cries:
When will you stop your nonsense?
But all the other children
are listening to the music
and the walls of the classroom
quietly dissolve.
The windows return to sand
the ink returns to water
the desks become trees again
the chalk goes back to being a cliff
the pen becomes, once more, a bird.

Histoire du Cheval by Jacques Prévert

tr. Irene Willis

THE HORSE'S STORY

Good people, hear my complaint.
Listen to the story of my life.
It is an orphan who speaks to you,
who tells you of his little woes—
so, here goes:
One day a general
or better, one *night*
it seems that a general
killed two of his horses.
These two horses were—
oh, my—how bitter life is—
my poor father
and my poor mother,
who were hidden under the bed,
under the bed of the general,
who was hidden in the rear
in a small town in the *Midi*.
The general was speaking—
was speaking all alone that night—
speaking, this general, of his little troubles
and that is how my father
and that is how my mother—oh, dear...
one night died of worry.
For me, family life was already over.

With a grand gallop, I ran away,
leaving in the night.
I ran off toward the big city,
where all was bright and shiny.
On a motorbike I arrived at *Sabi en Paro*
(Excuse me, I speak Horse).
One morning I arrived in Paris, wearing clogs
I demanded to see the lion,
King of the Beasts
and received a blow
on the corner of my nose,
for it was wartime.
The war was still going on
and I was stuck with blinders
to make me fit for war.
As the war continued
life would become dear,
life would diminish
and diminish more
and more as people gave me
funny looks
and clicked their teeth.
and that is the main thing.
Good evening,
good night.
Eat well, my general.

tr. Irene Willis

FAMILY LIFE

The mother knits.
The son makes war.
The mother finds this quite natural.
And the father, what does the father do?
He tends to business.
His wife knits.
His son makes war.
As for himself, he is all business.
The father finds this quite natural.
And the son, the son
what does the son find?
He finds nothing—absolutely nothing.
The son's mother knits, his father tends to business,
he makes war.
When the war is over
he will go into business with his father.
The war continues, the mother continues her knitting,
the father keeps tending to business.
The son is killed he does not continue.
The father and mother go to the cemetery.
They find this natural.
Life continues, life with knitting, war and business,
business, war and knitting, war,
business, business, business.

Le Message by Jacques Prévert

tr. Irene Willis

THE MESSAGE

The door that someone has opened
The door that someone has closed
The chair that someone is sitting in
The cat that someone has petted
The fruit that someone has bitten
The letter that someone has read
The chair that someone has turned around
The door that someone has opened
The road that someone has taken again
The wood that someone has crossed
The river where someone has thrown himself
The hospital where someone is dead

ACKNOWLEDGMENTS

As always, I would like to thank Olivia VanSant, P.A. *extraordinaire*, my wonderful computer consultant, Ernie Lowell, and my beloved Springer Spaniel, Abigail, who is somehow always with us, in spirit or as herself, when we work on anything connected with poems.

I am forever grateful for the supportive fellowship of Lisken Van Pelt Dus, Cynthia Gardner, Hilary Russell, Phil Timpane, our U.K. member, Chris Fogg, my morning poetry buddy, David Giannini, and the residents and staff at Devonshire Estates in Lenox, Massachusetts.

Gratitude also to Tamar and Larry Schwartz at IPBooks, for always being there and for doing whatever needs to be done, whenever.

NOTES:

Re: the poem "Lives of the Famous." Whittaker Chambers spent early years as a member of the Communist Party and Soviet Spy, then defected in 1938, worked for *Time* Magazine and then testified against them in 1949–50. This was the switch from left to right that became a metaphor in my poem. I worked for *Time* as a copygirl after graduating from high school and before going off to college.

A further note on this poem: One of my duties as undergraduate chair of the lecture series at SUNY Fredonia was to have dinner with the visiting lecturers at a local restaurant, courtesy of the university. They made no exception for Auden. "That's amazing! What on earth did you talk about?" one of my later mentors, Maxine Kumin, asked me." Never at a loss for conversational topics, I told her I had asked what he thought of the Charlie Chaplin scandals, which were all over the news at that time. Sadly, I don't remember what he replied, but we had a sprightly conversation, and he signed his portrait for me with my pen, which was filled with my schoolgirl green ink. Years later, I sold it to a rare books dealer for the princely sum of $75.00.

Re: the poem "Good Book." When my friend and mentor Alicia Ostriker was in China with her husband, a well-known astrophysicist, I wrote this poem in recognition of her work as a teacher of Judaic studies. To my shock, the e-mail was not to be sent; it bounced back with the words: *Banned Title.*

The poems "Tenement Year," "Her Cane" and "We Were Laughing Then" are dedicated to Irma Shulman Greene.

About the Author

Irene Willis has published five full-length poetry collections, plus an anthology of poems called *Climate of Opinion: Sigmund Freud in Poetry* (IPBooks, 2017) and another, co-edited with Jim Haba, called *What They Bring: The Poetry of Migration and Immigration* (IPBooks, 2020). Three times nominated for Pushcart Prizes and once for a National Book Award, her poems have also  appeared in many journals and anthologies. She has received a Distinguished Artist Fellowship from the New Jersey State Council on the Arts, a residency fellowship from the Millay Colony for the Arts, and grants from the Millay Colony for the Arts and the Berkshire/Taconic Foundation. She attended St. Lawrence University, holds a B.S. from SUNY Fredonia, an M.A. and Ph.D. from New York University and M.F.A. in Poetry from New England College. A longtime educator who has "retired" three times, she has taught in high schools, colleges and graduate schools, most recently at Westfield State University and American International College, both in Massachusetts. An Emeritus member of the Authors' Guild, she is Poetry Editor of www.internationalpsychoanalysis.net, where she has a monthly column called "Poetry Monday."

www.ingramcontent.com/pod-product-compliance
Lightning Source LLC
Chambersburg PA
CBHW071355120626
46546CB00002B/701